Fruit of the Spirit

YOU MIGHT BE A CHRISTIAN IF...

John B. Booth, Ed.D.

WESTBOW
PRESS®
A DIVISION OF THOMAS NELSON
& ZONDERVAN

WestBow Press books may be ordered through booksellers or by contacting:

WestBow Press
A Division of Thomas Nelson & Zondervan
1663 Liberty Drive
Bloomington, IN 47403
www.westbowpress.com
844-714-3454

ISBN: 978-1-6642-5623-1 (sc)
ISBN: 978-1-6642-5624-8 (e)

Library of Congress Control Number: 2022901808

Print information available on the last page.

WestBow Press rev. date: 2/25/2022

I dedicate this book to our Lord and Savior, Jesus Christ. I would also like to thank Holy Spirit for giving the book to me.

So you'll recognize them by their fruit.

—Matthew 7:20

FRUIT OF THE SPIRIT

Fruit: A natural product of a living thing. Fruit must grow and have time to ripen.

Spirit: The Holy Spirit; the third member of God's triune; God and Christ inside us.

Fruit of the Spirit: The divine character within us.

FRUIT OF THE SPIRIT: GALATIANS 5:22-23

Love: Love is from God. Everyone who chooses to love has been born of God and knows God. Love chooses to put aside one's own preferences, desires, and needs to put the other person first (1 Cor. 13:13; 1 Cor. 16:14; 1 Pet. 4:8; John 4:8).

Joy: Joy is gladness and delight in our inner spiritual selves. Joy comes from God and is not determined by our circumstances (1 Thess. 5:16; Phil. 4:4; 1 Pet. 1:8; Rom. 14:17).

Peace: We seek the spirit of Christ's peace no matter the circumstances. We have no worries, fears, or concerns (John 16–33; John 14:27; Phil. 4:6–7; 2 Thess. 3:16).

Patience: Patience is endurance, long-suffering, and perseverance (1 Cor. 13:4–5; Rom. 12:12; Eph. 4:2; Gal. 6:2).

Kindness: Kindness encompasses being generous, considerate, and friendly (Matt. 5:40–43; Luke 6:35; 2 Cor. 6:6; Col. 3:12).

Goodness: Goodness is righteousness in action and doing what is right even if there are consequences (Rom. 2:4; Gal. 6:10; Rom. 12:21; Rom. 12:9).

Faithfulness: Displaying faithfulness involves being reliable, trustworthy, and totally submissive to God (Mark 12:30; Rom. 8:28; 1 Cor. 2:9).

Gentleness: Gentleness is grace of the soul—not weakness but strength under control (James 3:17; Eph. 4:2; Heb. 13:1–2; Titus 3:1–2).

Self-control: Self-control is saying no to the flesh (1 Tim. 3:2–3; 2 Tim. 3:2; Titus 2:11–12; 2 Tim. 1:7).

Following the fruit of the spirit means choosing to have your faith, not your feelings, dictate your actions.

LOVE

Love is from God. Everyone who chooses to love has been born of God and knows God. Love chooses to put aside one's own preferences, desires, and needs to put the other person first (1 Cor. 13:13; 1 Cor. 16:14; 1 Pet. 4:8; John 4:8).

LOVE

You might be a Christian if …

> ➢ People look at you and say, "I want whatever they have!"

> ➢ The atmosphere of a room changes for the positive just by you entering.

> ➢ You can see the good in any individual.

> You cry when you see someone hurt.

> You have forgiven someone who has done you a terrible wrong.

> You allow Holy Spirit to guide you.

➤ You measure success by the closeness of your relationship with the Lord.

➤ You know the most important work you do today is to be a disciple of Jesus.

➤ You see the majesty of God in everything!

➤ You seek God first and foremost—not peace, joy, or even blessings.

➤ You understand it's not about sins; it's about sin.

➤ You don't just know *about* God; you know Him personally.

➢ You know you go to church with people who sin and are hypocritical, but you love them anyway because you are one of them.

➢ You understand that love isn't only an emotion you feel but also an action you choose.

JOY

Joy is gladness and delight in our inner spiritual selves. Joy comes from God and is not determined by our circumstances (1 Thess. 5:16; Phil. 4:4; 1 Pet.1:8; Rom. 14:17).

JOY

You might be a Christian if …

> ➤ You sing the loudest off-key praise music because you are singing to Him and not to anyone else.

> ➤ You see a beautiful sunrise and immediately praise God.

> ➤ You jump and shout praise for God louder than you jump and shout at a ball game.

➢ The first thing you say when you wake and the last thing you say at night is "Thank You, Lord."

➢ You sing and listen to praise music while washing dishes, mowing, buying groceries, or paying bills.

➢ You know the difference between happiness, an emotion, and joy, a state of being.

➢ You don't need alcohol or drugs to provide a "happy hour."

➢ You have the same kind of joy, excitement, and praise for Jesus as you do for a child as they take their first step.

➤ Your eyes and heart have been opened to the fact that your sins are forgiven.

➤ When something terrible happens in your life and you don't understand why, you still have a deep, abiding joy for our Lord.

PEACE

We seek the spirit of Christ's peace no matter the circumstances. We have no worries, fears, or concerns (John 16–33; John 14:27; Phil. 4:6–7; 2 Thess. 3:16).

PEACE

You might be a Christian if …

> After a great loss, you praise God.

> You pray for healing and actually expect healing.

> You are happy with who you are—no more and no less.

➢ You never get offended by anyone or anything.

➢ You have quiet time with the Lord every day.

➢ You are not concerned with the outcomes in life. You're concerned with following the lead of Holy Spirit.

➢ You are relaxed and content because you know you are following God's will.

➢ You are thankful for losing a job because you know He has something better headed your way.

➢ You realize that life will give you more than you can handle—but not more than God can handle for you.

➢ You find you get more done each day by starting the day being still with Jesus.

PATIENCE

Patience is endurance, long-suffering, and perseverance (1 Cor. 13:4–5; Rom. 12:12; Eph. 4:2; Gal. 6:2).

PATIENCE

You might be a Christian if …

> ➤ Someone cuts you off in traffic and you thank the Lord for safety and pray for that person.

> ➤ You ask God for something according to His will and you believe without a second thought that it will happen.

> ➤ When in a drive-through at a fast-food restaurant and the person in front of you changes the order three times and asks twenty questions, you praise God that you have extra time to talk to Him.

➢ You don't get upset by unbelievers when they don't understand you and think you are foolish.

➢ You pray for a miracle and expect it to happen.

➢ You pray for something for thirty years and still expect it to be fulfilled.

➤ You have asked your spouse to do something that is very important to you several times, and they continue to forget, but you love them anyway.

➤ You don't yell at your child when they make the same mistake for the umpteenth time.

➢ You allow Holy Spirit to give you peace when you have a plan and then there is one problem after another with the plan.

➢ You can say, "I don't remember the last time I lost my temper."

KINDNESS

Kindness encompasses being generous, considerate, and friendly (Matt. 5:40–43; Luke 6:35; 2 Cor. 6:6; Col. 3:12).

KINDNESS

You might be a Christian if …

> ➤ You see a homeless person for the third time in one day at the same intersection and you still give to them.

> ➤ You never say anything bad about another person.

> ➤ You give more than a tithe.

➢ You are in financial need but see someone in more need than you and give to them.

➢ One of the first things that comes to your mind is "How can I help?"

➢ You are known for going out of your way to help others, even strangers.

➢ You help someone even though they have publicly been hateful to you.

➢ You have something planned for the day, but you hear of a person in need and change your plans to help them.

➤ You are being kind to a person but the rest of your friends are saying, "How in the world can you be kind to that person after what they have done?"

➤ Random acts of kindness become as natural to you as breathing.

GOODNESS

Goodness is righteousness in action and doing what is right even if there are consequences (Rom. 2:4; Gal. 6:10; Rom. 12:21; Rom. 12:9).

GOODNESS

You might be a Christian if …

➤ You spend more time reading the Bible than watching TV.

➤ Someone has called you a "narrow-minded Bible thumper."

➤ You refuse to be embarrassed by the world for following God's Word.

➢ You continue to do good even when it seems to not matter.

➢ When you wake up in the morning, your main desire for the day is to make God happy.

➢ You spend more time praying for others than for yourself.

➢ You do the right thing even when you know there will be consequences.

➢ You help someone in need in a way no one else will ever know.

➢ You return money when the cashier gives you too much change.

➢ You drive the speed limit.

➢ You pray for your spouse, boss/job, government, and church instead of complaining about them.

➢ People chastise you because you are such a "rules follower."

FAITHFULNESS

Displaying faithfulness involves being reliable, trustworthy, and totally submissive to God (Mark 12:30; Rom. 8:28; 1 Cor. 2:9).

FAITHFULNESS

You might be a Christian if …

➢ You ask God for advice before you ask your neighbor.

➢ You figure out that the saying "God helps those who help themselves" is wrong. God helps those who come to Him.

➢ You realize a book titled *How to Improve Your Productivity* is called the Bible.

➢ You remain focused on God no matter what is happening around you.

➢ You spend more time thinking about Jesus than you do about politics or money.

➢ You know the perfect prayer doesn't come from what you read, write, or speak but from the heart.

➢ When you've been swallowed by a fish, you know that's not the end of the story.

➢ When someone asks you to do something for them and then something comes up that you would much rather do, you still honor your word.

➢ Someone says of you, "Their word is their bond" or "I've never heard them tell a lie."

➤ You understand that there could be a "Donated by Jesus Christ" sticker on everything you have: house, car, spouse, children, and so forth.

➤ You understand it is how you live and not what you profess that counts.

➤ You know you are a fully righteous child of God who sins *a lot*.

GENTLENESS

Gentleness is grace of the soul—not weakness but strength under control (James 3:17; Eph. 4:2; Heb. 13:1–2; Titus 3:1–2).

GENTLENESS

You might be a Christian if …

> You have changed from being a grouchy, self-centered person always wanting their own way into a humble, warm, forgiving soul.

> You have the humility to be last.

> You never refer to yourself in a conversation.

➢ You work hard on a project, yet you let someone else take the credit.

➢ No one notices you personally, but they notice the awesome person of God coming through you.

➢ Everyone you see you consider equal to or greater than you in the eyes of the Lord.

➢ You believe the practice of nonviolence requires a belief in divine vengeance.

➢ You don't mind being a doormat for Jesus to use.

➢ You don't "keep score" with your spouse.

➢ You have a hard time watching the news because there is so much pain and suffering shown in the world.

➢ The only thing you post on social media are affirming words of the gospel.

SELF-CONTROL

Self-control is saying no to the flesh (1 Tim. 3:2–3; 2 Tim. 3:2; Titus 2:11–12; 2 Tim. 1:7).

SELF-CONTROL

You might be a Christian if ...

> You show others the grace God has shown you.

> You bite your lip instead of biting off someone's head.

> You choose not to engage in a negative conversation about someone.

➢ Holy Spirit has guided you to fast for a day every week, and you are able to follow through.

➢ You hear a juicy bit of gossip and don't tell anyone.

➢ To you, an abundant life means a close relationship with Jesus and not health and wealth.

➤ You never say anything you wouldn't want on a billboard with your name beside it.

➤ When you read something on social media that is totally opposite of your value system, instead of blasting a response, you leave it alone.

➤ When something inappropriate pops up on social media, you click, "Hide post," so you won't see any more of those.

➢ When a significant person in your life says something hurtful, instead of responding in a harmful manner, you respond with the love from Holy Spirit.

➢ You give God your failures as well as your victories.

➢ You realize you are in a right relationship with Christ not because of your repentance but because of what Christ did on the cross.

➢ You know you #1 job is to make disciples.

BIBLE BOOK ABBREVIATIONS

Matthew—Matt.

Romans—Rom.

1 Corinthians—1 Cor.

2 Corinthians—2 Cor.

Galatians—Gal.

Ephesians—Eph.

Philippians—Phil.

Colossians—Col.

1 Thessalonians—1 Thess.

2 Thessalonians—2 Thess.

1 Timothy—1 Tim.

2 Timothy—2 Tim.

Philemon—Phil.

Hebrews—Heb.

1 Peter—1 Pet.

2 Peter—2 Pet.

Revelation—Rev.